Generative AI:

The Beginner's Guide

By

Dr Bienvenue Maula

CONTENTS

1. **Introduction to Generative AI**: In this chapter, you can introduce the concept of Generative AI and provide a brief history of its development. You can explain the difference between Generative AI and other types of AI, such as discriminative AI. You can also discuss the applications of Generative AI, such as image and speech synthesis, text generation, and music composition.

2. **Generative Models**: In this chapter, you can discuss the different types of Generative Models, such as autoregressive models, generative adversarial networks (GANs), and variational autoencoders (VAEs). You can explain the working of these models and their applications.

3. **Image Synthesis**: In this chapter, you can focus on Generative AI's application in Image Synthesis. You can discuss different techniques for image

generation, such as GANs and VAEs. You can also explain the use cases of image synthesis, such as generating realistic images of non-existent objects or people.

4. **Text Generation**: In this chapter, you can discuss the use of Generative AI for text generation. You can explain the working of language models, such as GPT and BERT, and their applications. You can also talk about the challenges in text generation, such as maintaining coherence and avoiding biases.

5. **Music Composition**: In this chapter, you can discuss the application of Generative AI in music composition. You can explain how Generative AI can help musicians and composers generate new melodies and rhythms. You can also discuss different techniques for music generation, such as using recurrent neural networks (RNNs) and deep belief networks (DBNs).

CHAPTER I: INTRODUCTION TO GENERATIVE AI

Generative AI is a subfield of artificial intelligence that focuses on creating algorithms and models that can generate new data, such as images, text, music, and even videos. Unlike other types of AI that are designed to classify or predict existing data, Generative AI focuses on the creation of new and original data that has never been seen before.

The development of Generative AI has been driven by the need for algorithms that can simulate human creativity and imagination. By using Generative AI, it is possible to create new and unique content that can be used in a wide range of applications, including video games, film, music, and digital art.

Generative AI refers to a category of artificial intelligence algorithms and models that can produce new content, such as images, text, audio, and even video, based on patterns learned from large amounts of training data.

Examples Of Generative AI:

1. Generative Adversarial Networks (GANs): GANs are a popular type of generative AI model that involves two neural networks working against each other: a generator and a discriminator. The generator creates new samples, and the discriminator tries to determine whether each sample is real or fake. Over time, the generator improves its output, and the discriminator becomes better at recognizing fakes, resulting in realistic images or other content.

Generative Adversarial Networks (GANs) are a type of machine learning model that are used to generate new data, such as images or videos. GANs consist of two neural networks: a generator and a discriminator.

The generator takes random noise as input and generates new data that is similar to the training data. The discriminator is trained to differentiate between real data from the training set and the generated data from the generator. The generator is trained to produce data that is similar enough to the real data that the discriminator cannot tell the difference.

During training, the generator and the discriminator play a game where the generator tries to produce data that can fool the discriminator, while the discriminator tries to correctly classify whether the data is real or generated. As training progresses, the generator learns to produce more realistic data, and the discriminator becomes better at distinguishing between real and generated data.

GANs have been used to generate realistic images, such as faces, landscapes, and objects, as well as to generate new music and text.

They have many potential applications, such as in art and design, entertainment, and data augmentation for machine learning tasks.

2. **Variational Autoencoders (VAEs):** VAEs are another type of generative AI model that uses deep learning to encode input data into a lower-dimensional latent space and then decode it back into the original format. VAEs can be used to generate new data that is similar to the input data.

3. **Recurrent Neural Networks (RNNs):** RNNs are a type of neural network that can be used for text generation. They work by predicting the next word in a sequence based on the previous words, generating new sentences or even entire paragraphs.

4. **DeepDream:** DeepDream is a neural network visualization tool that can create psychedelic, surreal images by modifying existing images. It works by

enha ncing the patterns and structures that the neural network recognizes in the input image.

5. **MuseNet: MuseNet** is a generative model developed by OpenAI that can produce music in a variety of styles, from classical to jazz to rock. The model was trained on a large dataset of MIDI files and can generate entirely new compositions based on user inputs.

Generative AI has numerous practical applications, including content generation, artistic creation, and data augmentation for machine learning. However, it also raises concerns about the potential misuse of generated content and the impact on the job market.

Generative AI is based on several types of models, including Generative Adversarial Networks (GANs), Variational Autoencoders (VAEs), and autoregressive models. These models use complex algorithms and deep neural networks to generate new data that is similar to the training data. The training data can be a set of images, text, or other types of data that are used to train the model to **generate new data.**

The applications of Generative AI are numerous and continue to expand. For example, Generative AI can be used to create realistic images of objects that do not exist in the real world, to generate new and unique pieces of music, to create text that mimics human writing, and even to develop new virtual characters for use in video games and other digital media.

As the field of Generative AI continues to develop, it has the potential to revolutionize the way we think about creativity and the generation of new content. By enabling machines to create new and original data, Generative AI has the potential to open up new frontiers in art, entertainment, and communication.

A Brief History of Generative AI

The roots of Generative AI can be traced back to the early days of computing when researchers first began exploring the idea of creating machines that could think and create. One of the earliest examples of Generative AI is the work of British mathematician Alan Turing, who in the 1950s proposed the idea of a machine that could simulate any human thought process.

In the 1960s, researchers began to experiment with early forms of neural networks and machine learning, paving the way for the development of more sophisticated models capable of generating new data. In the 1980s, researchers began to explore the idea of creating generative models using Markov Chain Monte Carlo methods, which enabled the generation of new data from a probability distribution.

In the **1990s**, the development of Bayesian networks and graphical models led to new techniques for modeling complex data and generating new content. In the early 2000s, researchers began to experiment with deep neural networks and unsupervised learning techniques, which led to the development of advanced Generative AI models capable of generating highly realistic images, text, and music.

One of the most significant breakthroughs in Generative AI came in 2014 with the development of Generative Adversarial Networks (GANs) by Ian Goodfellow and his colleagues at the University of Montreal. GANs consist of two neural networks, one generator and one discriminator, which work together to generate new data that is highly realistic and difficult to distinguish from real data.

Since then, Generative AI has continued to evolve and has become a rapidly growing area of research and development. With the advent of new deep learning techniques and massive amounts of data available for training, the potential applications of Generative AI are vast and continue to expand. From art and entertainment to medicine and scientific research, Generative AI has the potential to transform the way we create and interact with digital content.

CHAPTER II: GENERATIVE MODELS

Generative models are a class of machine learning algorithms that are used to generate new, previously unseen data that resembles a given training dataset. These models can be used to generate new images, videos, audio, text, and other types of data.

Generative models work by learning the underlying distribution of the training data, and then using this distribution to generate new samples. There are several types of generative models, including:

1. **Variational Autoencoders (VAEs):** VAEs are a type of neural network that learns a low-dimensional representation of the input data, called the latent space, and

can then generate new data by sampling from this space.

2. **Generative Adversarial Networks (GANs):** GANs consist of two neural networks, a generator and a discriminator. The generator generates new samples, while the discriminator tries to distinguish between real and generated samples. The two networks are trained together, with the generator trying to fool the discriminator, and the discriminator trying to correctly identify the generated samples.

3. **Autoregressive models:** Autoregressive models generate new data by modeling the probability distribution of each element in the sequence, conditioned on the previous elements.

Generative models have many applications, including image and video synthesis, data augmentation, text generation, and drug discovery. However, generating high-quality samples can be a challenging task, and the generated data may not always be indistinguishable from real data.

Variational Autoencoders (VAEs) are a type of generative model that learn to encode and decode data. They are widely used in applications such as image and audio generation, data compression, and data denoising. Here are some examples of VAEs:

1. **Image Generation**: VAEs can be used to generate realistic images from random noise. One example of this is the DALL-E model developed by OpenAI, which generates images from textual descriptions using a VAE architecture.
2. **Anomaly Detection**: VAEs can be trained to learn a distribution of normal data and then detect anomalies in new data. This can be used for applications such as fraud detection or identifying defects in manufacturing.

3. **Denoising**: VAEs can be trained to reconstruct noisy data by learning a lower-dimensional representation of the clean data. This can be used to remove noise from images or audio signals.

4. **Unsupervised Learning**: VAEs can be used for unsupervised learning, where the model learns to represent the data without any labeled examples. This can be useful for exploratory data analysis or feature extraction.

5. **Video Generation**: VAEs can also be used to generate videos by modeling the spatiotemporal structure of the data. This can be used for applications such as video synthesis or video prediction.

These are just a few examples of the many applications of VAEs. VAEs are a versatile type of generative model that can be adapted to many different types of data and applications.

Generative Adversarial Networks (GANs) are a type of generative model that consist of two neural networks: a generator and a discriminator. The generator network learns to create new data that is similar to the training data, while the discriminator network learns to distinguish between the generated data and the real data. The two networks are trained together in a adversarial setting, where the generator tries to produce realistic data that can fool the discriminator, while the discriminator tries to correctly identify whether the data is real or fake.

Here are some examples of applications of GANs:

1. **Image Generation**: GANs are commonly used to generate realistic images that resemble the training data. One example of this is StyleGAN, which can generate high-resolution images of faces that look like real people.
2. Data Augmentation: GANs can be used to generate additional training data for

machine learning models, which can improve their accuracy. For example, a GAN can be trained on a small dataset of images and then generate new images that can be added to the training set.

3. **Image Editing**: GANs can be used to perform image-to-image translation, where an input image is transformed into a different style or appearance. For example, a GAN can be used to transform a photograph into a painting or to change the color of an object in an image.

4. **Text-to-Image Synthesis**: GANs can be used to generate images from textual descriptions. This involves training a GAN on pairs of text and image data, so that it can learn to generate images that match the descriptions.

5. Video Synthesis: GANs can be used to generate videos by generating each frame of the video independently. This can be used to create realistic

animations or to generate new video content based on existing footage.

These are just a few examples of the many applications of GANs. GANs are a powerful tool for generating new data and creating novel content, and they have many potential applications in fields such as art, design, and entertainment.

Autoregressive models are a type of statistical model that are used to model time series data or sequences, where the prediction of each value depends on the previous values. Here's an example of an autoregressive model:

1. **Language Modeling**: Language models are a type of autoregressive model that are used to generate text. These models predict the next word in a sentence based on the previous words. One example of this is the GPT (Generative Pre-trained Transformer) model developed by OpenAI, which is a

transformer-based autoregressive model that can generate coherent and fluent text.

2. **Time Series Analysis**: Autoregressive models are commonly used in time series analysis to predict future values based on past values. One example of this is the ARIMA (Autoregressive Integrated Moving Average) model, which is a type of linear autoregressive model that can be used to predict future values of a time series.

3. **Music Generation**: Autoregressive models can also be used to generate music. These models predict the next note in a sequence based on the previous notes. One example of this is the Music Transformer model developed by Google, which is a transformer-based autoregressive model that can generate realistic and diverse music.

4. **Video Synthesis**: Autoregressive models can be used to generate videos by

generating each frame of the video based on the previous frames. One example of this is the Video Transformer model developed by Google, which is a transformer-based autoregressive model that can generate high-quality video sequences.

5. **Image Generation**: Autoregressive models can also be used to generate images by predicting the next pixel value based on the previous pixels. One example of this is the PixelCNN model, which is an autoregressive model that can generate high-quality images one pixel at a time.

These are just a few examples of the many applications of autoregressive models. Autoregressive models are a powerful tool for modeling sequences and generating new data, and they have many potential applications in fields such as language processing, music, and video synthesis.

CHAPTER III: IMAGE SYNTHESIS

Image synthesis is one of the most popular applications of autoregressive models. Autoregressive models are used to generate new images pixel by pixel, where the model predicts each pixel based on the previous pixels. The generated images can be used for a variety of purposes, including artistic expression, data augmentation, and computer vision.

Here are some examples of autoregressive models for image synthesis:

1. **PixelRNN and PixelCNN**: These models are the first successful autoregressive models for image synthesis. They model the probability distribution of each pixel given the previous pixels in a row-by-row or column-by-column fashion, respectively. PixelRNN and PixelCNN can

generate high-quality images, but they are computationally expensive and slow.

2. **WaveNet**: WaveNet is an autoregressive model originally developed for speech synthesis, but it has also been used for image synthesis. The model predicts the next pixel in an image based on a stack of dilated convolutional layers. WaveNet can generate high-quality images with fewer parameters than PixelRNN and PixelCNN.

3. **Conditional PixelCNN**: This model is an extension of PixelCNN that can generate images based on a given condition, such as a class label or a textual description. The model combines the condition with the previous pixels to predict the next pixel.

4. Gated PixelCNN: This model is an extension of PixelCNN that introduces a gating mechanism to improve the quality of generated images. The gating mechanism controls the flow of

information between the vertical and horizontal directions of the image.

5. **Glow**: Glow is an autoregressive flow-based model that can generate high-quality images with a more efficient architecture than PixelRNN and PixelCNN. The model uses invertible 1x1 convolutions and affine coupling layers to generate images.

These are just a few examples of the many autoregressive models for image synthesis. Autoregressive models have been used to generate a wide range of images, including faces, animals, landscapes, and more. They have also been combined with other techniques such as GANs to improve the quality and diversity of generated images.

PixelRNN and PixelCNN

PixelRNN and **PixelCNN** are both autoregressive models for image synthesis that model the probability distribution of each pixel given the previous pixels. PixelRNN models the probability distribution of each row of pixels in an image sequentially from left to right, while PixelCNN models the probability distribution of each pixel based on the previous pixels in a row and a column. Here are some examples of each model:

1. **PixelRNN**: The original PixelRNN model was trained on the CIFAR-10 dataset, which consists of 32x32 color images of 10 classes. The model was able to generate realistic images of objects such as airplanes, cars, and cats. Here's an example of an image generated by PixelRNN:

3. **PixelCNN++**: PixelCNN++ is an improved version of PixelCNN that uses a larger receptive field to capture more context information. The model was trained on the ImageNet dataset, which consists of high-resolution images of various classes. PixelCNN++ was able to generate high-quality images of natural scenes, animals, and objects.

WaveNet

a stack of dilated convolutional layers. Here are some examples of the WaveNet model for image synthesis:

1. **ImageNet**: WaveNet was trained on the ImageNet dataset, which consists of high-resolution images of various classes. The model was able to generate high-quality images with fine details and natural textures.

CelebA: WaveNet was also trained on the CelebA dataset, which consists of high-resolution images of celebrity faces. The model was able to generate high-quality images of faces with realistic facial features such as eyes, nose, and mouth.

WaveNet was trained on a dataset of anime images, which consists of cartoon-style images with bright colors and bold outlines. The model was able to generate anime-style images with fine details and vivid colors.

CHAPTER IV: TEXT GENERATION

Text generation is a common application of autoregressive models, and one popular model for this task is the GPT (Generative Pre-trained Transformer) family of models. Here's an example of GPT-2 for text generation:

1. **Language Modeling**: GPT-2 was trained on a large corpus of text, and it is capable of generating coherent and fluent text in a variety of styles and genres. Here's an example of a short story generated by GPT-2:

```vbnet
Once upon a time, in a faraway land, there was a young princess named Lily. She had

However, their happiness was short-lived. The evil sorcerer who ruled the land was

Determined to save his beloved, the prince set out on a perilous journey to the lan
```

This example shows how GPT-2 can generate a coherent and engaging story that follows a traditional fairytale structure.

2. **Question-Answering**: GPT-3, the latest and largest model in the GPT family, has been trained on a variety of tasks including question-answering. Here's an example of a question and answer generated by GPT-3:

Question: Who was the first president of the United States?

Answer: George Washington was the first president of the United States. He served two terms from 1789 to 1797.

This example shows how GPT-3 can generate accurate and informative responses to factual questions.

3. **Chatbot**: GPT-3 has also been used to create chatbots that can simulate human-like conversation. Here's an

example of a conversation with a GPT-3 chatbot:

User: Hi, how are you today?

Chatbot: I'm doing well, thank you for asking. How can I assist you?

User: Can you recommend a good restaurant in the area?

Chatbot: Sure, I can help with that. What type of cuisine are you in the mood for?

User: How about Italian?

Chatbot: Great, there's a popular Italian restaurant called Piazza Italia that I can recommend. It's known for its homemade pasta and authentic Italian flavors.

This example shows how GPT-3 can generate natural and engaging responses to user queries in a chatbot setting.

These examples demonstrate the versatility of GPT models for various natural language processing tasks, including language modeling, question-answering, and chatbot dialogue. GPT models have also been used for other tasks such as summarization, translation, and sentiment analysis.

CHAPTER VI: MUSIC COMPOSITION

Music composition is the process of creating new music, either by combining existing musical elements or by inventing new musical ideas. Traditionally, music composition has been the domain of human composers, who draw on their knowledge and experience of music theory, performance, and aesthetics to create works that express their unique artistic vision.

In recent years, machine learning techniques, such as autoregressive models, have been applied to the task of music composition. These models are trained on large datasets of existing music and can learn to generate new compositions that exhibit similar patterns and structures to the training data.

Autoregressive models for music composition typically work by generating one note or chord at a time, based on the sequence of notes that have come before. For example, a model might generate a melody note by note, with each note dependent on the notes that came before it. The resulting composition is therefore an autoregressive sequence, where each note or chord is conditioned on the previous ones.

One important challenge in using autoregressive models for music composition is generating music that is musically coherent and pleasing to the human ear. This requires the model to capture important aspects of musical structure, such as melody, harmony, and rhythm, and to balance these elements in a way that is both interesting and aesthetically pleasing.

Despite these challenges, autoregressive models for music composition have shown promising results, and have been used to generate new compositions in a variety of musical styles and genres. For example, some models have been trained to generate classical music, while others have been trained to create new sounds and rhythms in electronic music.

Overall, the application of machine learning to music composition is an exciting area of research that has the potential to expand the boundaries of what is possible in music and to open up new avenues for artistic expression.

One example of an autoregressive model used for music composition is the Performance RNN, a recurrent neural network developed by Google Magenta. The Performance RNN was trained on a large dataset of MIDI files, which are a type of digital music file that contains information about the notes, timing, and other characteristics of a musical performance.

The Performance RNN is capable of generating new musical compositions in a variety of styles, such as classical, jazz, and pop.

This example demonstrates how the Performance RNN can generate music that is musically coherent and follows the patterns and structures of a particular genre or style.

Another example of an autoregressive model used for music composition is the WaveNet-based **sampleRNN model** developed by the University of Montreal. This model uses a combination of autoregressive and hierarchical modeling techniques to generate music. It was trained on a large dataset of audio samples, such as notes played by different musical instruments.

The sampleRNN is capable of generating new musical compositions with a high degree of detail and fidelity.

This example demonstrates how the sampleRNN can generate music with a high degree of complexity and variation, and can create new sounds that are not necessarily limited by existing musical genres or conventions.

Vocabulary

1. **Generative model**: A type of AI model that is capable of generating new data, such as images, music, or text.

2. **Autoregressive model**: A type of generative model that predicts the next element in a sequence based on the previous elements in the sequence.

3. **Variational Autoencoder (VAE)**: A type of generative model that learns to encode and decode data in a latent space, allowing it to generate new data that is similar to the training data.

4. **Generative Adversarial Network (GAN)**: A type of generative model that consists of two neural networks, one of which generates data and the other of which tries to distinguish between real and fake data.

5. **PixelRNN and PixelCNN**: Two types of autoregressive models that generate images pixel by pixel.

6. **WaveNet:** An autoregressive model that is used for generating audio.
7. Autoregressive language model: A type of autoregressive model that is used for generating text.
8. **Image synthesis:** The task of generating new images using AI models.
9. Music composition: The task of creating new music using AI models.
10. **Text generation:** The task of creating new text using AI models.